housebeautiful
Lighting

Inspiring Ideas for Lighting Effects, From Simple to Spectacular

The Editors of House Beautiful Magazine

Text by
Judith Gura

HEARST BOOKS   NEW YORK

Library of Congress Cataloging-in-Publication Data

House beautiful : lighting / by the editors of House beautiful.
    p. cm.
  ISBN 1-58816-101-3
    1. Lighting, Architectural and decorative. 2. Interior decoration.
    I. Title: Lighting. II. House beautiful.
  NK2115.5.L5 H68 2002
  729'.28--dc21

2001039697

Printed in China

FIRST EDITION

1 2 3 4 5 6 7 8 9 10

Edited by Laurie Orseck
Designed by Susi Oberhelman

produced by smallwood & stewart, inc., new york, ny

www.housebeautiful.com

CONTENTS

We are inclined to take light for granted. It is everywhere around us, shaping our lives and enabling us to see. And electricity places it entirely at our command. But that was not always the case. Although electricity has been around as long as the earth itself, it was not until the nineteenth century that scientists learned to harness it for the creation of light. Through their efforts, light allows us to control our surroundings.

Defining light is at once very simple and impossibly complex. Light is energy, the movement of electrons that stimulate our visual receptors. It has no mass, no volume. As vital as the air we breathe, it affects the mind, the body, and the emotions. We tend to be cheerful on sunny days and gloomy on cloudy ones; energetic by day and sleepy at night; warm and secure in a bright room and unsettled in a darkly shadowed one. Scientific studies indicate that humans need at least two hours of light exposure each day to function normally; without it, our productivity decreases and we lose a sense of well-being. Vital to sustenance, light is also linked to our most pleasant experiences—the warmth of a fire, the glow of a sunset, the spotlight on a stage. Small wonder, then, that when deprived of light from nature, man creates it for himself.

Light has existed since the beginning of the universe—the direct light of the sun and the reflected light of the moon. But these were not altogether reliable, nor could they be controlled. Over the millennia of human existence, man has looked for ways to duplicate or supplement these natural sources of light, from the bare-walled cave to the window-walled skyscraper, with a combination of ingenuity and chance.

The primitive man who picked a burning brand out of a fire more than a million years ago invented the first portable light. This was fine for exploring caves and forests, but inconvenient, and even risky, for regular lighting indoors, so the search for a more controllable light source continued. Centuries later, an anonymous inventor in the ancient world placed an olive-oil-soaked wick in a clay container to create the first stationary lamp. Candles, a Roman invention, were less bright but more convenient than oil lamps, hearths, or primitive pine torches. By the Middle Ages, candelabra, candle-fitted wall sconces, and chandeliers provided decoration as well as illumination in grand cathedrals and great halls.

Over the next few centuries, great thinkers and scientists such as Leonardo da Vinci, René Descartes, Isaac Newton, and Albert Einstein explored the mysteries of light, and many others labored to find more efficient ways to light the home. By the end of the nineteenth century, gaslight, fueled by kerosene, was the most commonly used form of illumination in the home. All of this, however, would be pushed aside by a revolutionary development—electricity. In 1809, Englishman Humphry Davy passed electric current through two wires joined by a strip of charcoal, thus inventing the arc lamp, the ancestor of Thomas Edison's 1879 electric light bulb, and heralding the modern age of lighting.

Today, we can enjoy two kinds of light, natural and artificial, one a gift of nature, the other a boon of technology. The first is not entirely within our control, but the second enables us to control our environment. The specific types of artificial light we choose, and the ways in which we distribute it through the home, determine how these spaces feel, and how we feel in them. Using light effectively not only enables us to see but energizes our experience of living.

Complex lighting solutions are often best left to experts: a professional interior designer, or a lighting specialist. But some understanding of how light works and how it can be used will benefit even the "unenlightened" layman. Benjamin Franklin once said, "I am much in the dark about light." We hope *House Beautiful Lighting* will serve as a guide to some of the ways in which we can manipulate light to enhance our interiors and enrich our lives.

The sun is a constant; its light does not vary. But the earth is always moving, of course, so our perception of sunlight does vary according to our location on earth, the time of day, the season, and changes in the atmosphere. The exposures in every house or apartment determine both the quality and the amount of light

TING

day to night

that enters each room. A northern exposure—the traditional choice for the artist's studio—provides clear, consistent light from a reflective sky, with a cool, bluish cast that can seem chilly in winter. Eastern exposures have balanced, brighter morning sunlight, though they can be subject to glare. The light from the west is warm, even physically hot, but hazy from impurities in the afternoon air. South-facing windows, the favorite source of natural light, admit warm sunlight for the longest period each day, all year long.

Despite the constancy of its source, the light that enters through our windows varies in intensity, direction, and coloration as it moves through a space in the course of the day. It is, in fact, the only element of an interior scheme that changes continuously. Although daylight is a random mix of light of all wavelengths, it is not actually consistent. At dawn or sunset, it has few blue-green tones, making it appear reddish to the eye. Conversely, cloudy days rob it of its red-orange tones, resulting in a bluish cast. Daylight is influenced by variations in geography, climate, and circumstance as well. Streaming into a room, it interacts with other elements, changing its own appearance and theirs. Light diffused through curtains, shadows cast by shutters, reflections from white walls and polished surfaces create colors and patterns of their own. Light at dawn can be almost mauve; noon light is a glare-producing brilliant yellowish-white, afternoon light glows with gold, and sunset introduces a duskiness that can alternate between moody and murky.

Taking advantage of a sunny exposure, designer Samantha Cole created a circular breakfast room (opposite) to bring the garden view inside. The faux-tented ceiling, trompe l'oeil foliage, and outdoor-style awnings re-create the early-day mood, even after dark. Above: Morning sun casts evocative shadows over sand-colored floors and light furnishings in the dining area of Steven and Marlo Ehrlich's Santa Monica beach house.

Creamy walls reflect the warm southern light in a Charleston, South Carolina, living room by designer Amelia T. Handegan (above). The coolness of pale-toned carpeting and upholstery is set off by a hand-painted screen. Opposite: In a modern wing designed by architects Susan Lanier and Paul Lubowicki for a Spanish Colonial house in Los Angeles, a soaring expanse of glass opens onto the garden, bringing in every possible ray of natural light. At night, warm interior lighting takes its place.

Still, even with its variable nature, natural light is the kind we find most appealing. It shows colors and textures at their most attractive and most familiar, and it is energy-efficient. The ideal lighting plan would illuminate every room from sunrise to sundown with its clear, balanced, evenly distributed magic. That, of course, is impossible. In reality, we need to control heat and glare, to diffuse or screen out direct sunlight, to dim rooms for atmosphere and darken them for sleeping. Though we can alter the size and location of windows and install skylights to admit more natural light, these options are costly and not always feasible. The challenge is to make the most of every ray of sunlight in settings just cool enough for comfortable living.

Designing a realistic lighting plan, then, involves both manipulating the available light from natural sources and supplementing or simulating it with man-made substitutes: artificial light, window treatments, surfaces that diffuse and reflect. The lighting that results should be neither too bright nor too dull, neither too diffused nor too flat. It should create a feeling of vitality while sustaining one of calm. It should enter a space from more than one direction—above, below, even angled to play light against shadows. And the happy outcome should be an environment that is aesthetically pleasing and emotionally warming, rooms and spaces in which we feel welcome and comfortable at any time of day or night.

The early rays of the sun are often the most desirable—not too hot, and not too harsh in color. Rooms with natural morning light rarely need any artificial supplements until much later in the day.

In this Connecticut cottage, morning sunlight streams in through a row of old-fashioned windows, whose mullioned squares cast pretty shadows as the sun moves on. Lynn Morgan designed the wainscoted living room with a Scandinavian look: a fresh blue-and-white color scheme that's round-the-clock cool, whitewashed beams that make the most of the ceiling height, and furniture that bespeaks curl-up-and-relax comfort. Unobtrusive halogen down-lights strung between the beams make the room just as inviting after dark. Their white-toned lighting, more appropriate here than incandescent bulbs, re-create the feeling of waking up to a bright new day.

Overleaf: Afternoon light sends flattering shadows onto walls and furniture (left). The sunny bedroom (right), in the same blue-and-white scheme, relies on linen-shaded windows to diffuse daylight, and adjustable brass wall lamps for reading in bed.

White is the best reflector of natural light, but bright furnishings in daylight-rich interiors can actually enhance the quality of light in a room. This lively New Orleans living room admits the light through tall bay windows, wisely left entirely bare. The vibrant-toned upholstery looks good at any hour, and its juicy citrus hues loosen up the formality of the classical architecture.

More designers and architects are planning interiors around available natural light, and they're giving more attention to the windows that bring it in.

Left: White curtains and wraparound white walls make the tall French doors in a casual traditional dining room seem wider. Opposite: John Saladino designed an inviting porch-turned-solarium in a Connecticut country house so that its main attraction is two walls of windows. Banquette-style seating nestles just beneath the sills, and Roman shades can be lowered to filter the sun.

Los Angeles designer Kerry Joyce hits all the right notes in a Beverly Hills home by balancing a white-on-white environment with warm-toned wood floors. Lots of windows and French doors, framing views of leafy, landscaped gardens, allow the space to be saturated with light. In the living room (opposite), windows are left bare, and the all-white scheme is textured with beige and creamy tones. The kitchen and dining area (right) are flooded with light through a wall of French doors. Supplementary lighting is recessed into the tongue-and-groove wood-plank ceiling.

Overleaf: Opening to the patio, another wall of windows and doors allows the outdoors to flow inside. White furnishings are set off by very dark woods; the moldings and beamed ceiling keep the scheme from being stark.

By afternoon, the sun is at its warmest, the light is at its most intense, and the potential for damage to furniture, rugs, and artwork is greatest. Rooms that receive strong afternoon sunlight should have protective window coverings. Visual side effects are another consideration: In afternoon light, particularly from western exposures, too much yellow may visually overheat a room's decor.

Opposite: Stuart Schepps designed an inviting living room, with marine-blue walls and toned-down lighting, that is cool enough to accommodate a lacquer-red painting. A leaded glass screen in front of the tall curtained window provides extra insurance against the light. Natural materials such as wicker and raffia and a vegetable-dyed rug are ecofriendly hints of the outdoors. Right: A luminous Paris apartment glows from day into night. Designer-owner Mary Shaw chose buttery yellow walls that extend the quality of the afternoon light without being too intense, then cooled them off with white moldings, a white fireplace surround, and mostly neutral-toned textured fabrics.

color and light

Light and color are interdependent and inextricably linked. It is through the stimulus of light on the retina that we perceive color, and our perception is affected by the characteristics of the light. If light were perfectly balanced, there would be no effect at all, but even natural daylight, a mixture of wavelengths containing the entire spectrum of color, varies with the time of day. As daylight takes on a cast of red or blue or gold, so do the colors of the objects we see. The eye, however, adapts to these changes, and we barely notice them.

Variations in artificial light can be more disturbing. Some tones of light cause us to misperceive or misjudge colors; almost everyone has dressed under incandescent light, only to go outdoors and find that two items of clothing don't actually match. Colors are also modified by reflections from surrounding objects, and the same colors on different surfaces or materials reflect or absorb light differently. Despite such variations, we recognize colors for what they are, but they may not look their best. Selecting the amount and quality of illumination to render colors as accurately as possible is the goal of every lighting scheme.

Since it's not practical to keep moving furniture just to show it in a better light, a lighting plan must take into account the colors of furnishings and interior surfaces as well as the lighting requirements of the room. But the reverse is also true, in that the colors of walls and furnishings can enhance or detract from the existing light or can help to compensate for its deficiencies.

When working with light and color, a few guidelines will help ensure the best possible results:

■ Before buying paint, fabric, or floor covering, check the colors where they will be used, under both day and evening light. No two examples of a single color are exactly alike—not all yellows are hot, nor all blues cool—and hues may change under different lights and even in different locations in the same room.

■ Except for rooms used mostly at night, take the exposure into consideration. Bluish morning light may need the balance of warm color (in auxiliary lighting as well as furnishings); a sunlight-flooded space may benefit from a dash of cools.

■ Generally speaking, colors are flattered by lighting in which similar hues predominate: Incandescent light makes yellows more glowing, reds richer, and oranges juicier; daylight bulbs enhance blues and greens. Conversely, light with tones from the opposite side of the color wheel tend to distort or muddy a given hue. Halogen lighting shows intense colors at their best, so it is generally the most flattering choice for a lively, multicolor scheme.

■ White walls are natural reflectors that flatter any color of furnishings, as well as enhancing the effects of both natural and artificial light. Even in the absence of other hues, white is never boring; it changes with the gradual shadings of natural light. Lighting in a white room should compensate for these changes.

- Color values are best rendered in a room where there is plenty of good, evenly distributed lighting.
- In cases of poor natural light, halogen—cooler but clearer than incandescent, warmer than fluorescent—is a good solution, as it is most like direct sunlight.
- Use cool-toned light at high levels of illumination and warm tones at lower ones. This suggests halogen for brightly lit interiors, and incandescent or candlelight for low-lit rooms. These choices are not only more comfortable to the eye, but also ensure more accurate rendering of colors as the light changes through the day.
- Full-spectrum lighting, which contains the full range of colors that exist in daylight, renders colors more accurately than any other light and is considered psychologically beneficial.

Windows that face south are blessed with all-season sunlight that sets interiors aglow, flattering every furniture style. All colors look good in this type of environment; in such a forgiving setting, it's hard to make a poor design choice.

A small San Francisco apartment (opposite) enjoys the pleasures of a wraparound view thanks to almost floor-to-ceiling windows that expand the space of its 20-foot-long oval living room. Designer-owner Paul Wiseman used tone-on-tone yellow walls that mimic the fading rays of sunlight, and dressed the room in fine but unmatched neoclassical furniture linked by upholstery in harmonizing tones. The grid of the windows adds a design element without blocking light or views and prevents their bareness from looking stark.

The Chinese Pavilion

INTERIOR VISIONS

IN THE ROMANTIC STYLE

WHITE

White walls present few decorating challenges, make any space look larger, and reflect both natural and artificial light. All shades of white, however, are not created equal; they can be warm or cold, dull or bright. In fact many light-conscious rooms are painted several shades of white— one for ceiling, one or more for walls, still another for moldings and trim. Choosing different tones and textures for walls, floors, and upholstery prevents a flat look that can come with an unrelieved white interior.

A light-filled dining room designed by DeBare Saunders and Ronald Mayne (opposite) only looks all white. Ethereal gray-green walls and floaty white silk over seafoam green chiffon at the windows are a subtle contrast to the pure white moldings and ceiling. At night, an antique chandelier creates a dramatic faux-candlelight effect. Right: In an 1840s tavern-turned-weekend house in Pennsylvania, several shades of warm white enrich the tones of antique and flea market wood furnishings. The light from a birdcage fitted with candles is augmented by a recessed ceiling fixture.

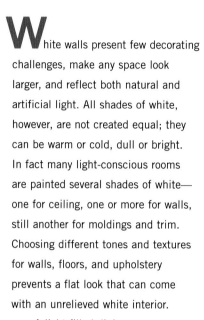

In a weekend home in upstate New York (opposite), architects Ann Kalla and Pietro Cicognani teamed up with interior designers Laura Bohn and Joseph Lembo to create a rustic retreat with Old World Italian charm and modern-day convenience. The blue-and-white color scheme of the living room flatters the crisp daylight from windows opposite the fireplace wall. After dark, concealed lighting softens the space. Right: A fourteenth-century English manor house inspired Mallory Marshall and James Light's stone retreat on the coast of Maine. Tall arches let light into the colonnade, which frames an open-air dining room, but it is heavily shaded by the overhanging roof. Unobtrusive downlights and an antique lantern compensate for the darkness of the wood.

A spectacular cathedral-ceilinged living room focuses on an overscale Gothic-style window. The formal seating arrangement is all `pastels that look equally pretty after dark. The pink-shaded chandelier, double-tiered to suit the grand scale and lighting needs of the space, is central to the evening plan. Wall sconces and a large decorative mirror multiply the glow.

Overleaf: The house's minimally windowed game room (left) is dressed in deep tones for evening and illuminated by several sources: wall-mounted sconces, a triple-shaded fixture hung low over the pool table, and conventional shaded reading lamps. In the dining room (right), walls of French doors admit light during the day, but because the room is used mostly at night, the window treatment is elaborate: Layers of white curtains and lengths of rich red drapery are repeated in shaded stripes on the ceiling. An antique chandelier with white parchment shades and blood-red glass drops echoes the sconces on the surrounding walls.

In true loft spaces, often all the windows are along only one wall. If a second exposure exists, it may face an air shaft or a similarly undesirable view. This creates both lighting and ventilation challenges. Another consideration is the presence of original brickwork and beams, which tend to darken a space. Lighting in lofts and loftlike interiors, therefore, is almost as critical as the placement of interior walls.

In the main living area of a downtown New York loft, new steel-framed windows with simple white shades replace the antiquated multipaned originals. They work in tandem with suspended ceiling floodlights to supply primary lighting in the multi-purpose space. Added illumination, as well as decorative interest, comes from several designer-styled vintage lamps that complement the midcentury furniture classics, and the warm color scheme enhances the wood beams and built-ins.

Overleaf: The loft's dining platform and kitchen area are a sleek addition, wrapped in pale polished wood and lit by a modern chandelier and a scattering of diminutive suspended spots.

Any place blessed with outdoor space should have at least one area designed to take advantage of it, no matter what the weather. In this Chicago home designed by Bobby McAlpine, an enclosed dining porch serves as an entryway to the greenery beyond. To underscore the intent of the room, the bluestone floor and simple furnishings have a greenish cast. Ceiling-height screens, topped by louvered transoms, wrap around the room, inviting in sunlight and fresh air through most of the day. In the evening, candles and parchment-shaded lamps supply the glow.

GREEN LIGHT

One of the major challenges of white interiors is to make them look good in different kinds of light. A room that is brilliantly crisp and clear by day can take on an unfortunate dull cast under artificial light. A white-on-white room requires lighting flexibility to look appealing at any hour.

All the right decisions were made in designing the light-filled, white-filled interiors of this New York City high-rise apartment, whose spectacular three walls of windows were offset by an awkward arrangement of rooms. Architects Peter Shelton and Lee Mindel reconfigured the plan, knocking down walls and creating a central core for utilities, which opened the space to dramatic city views and dawn-to-dusk natural light. Then they devised a single-color scheme with varying tones and textures that reflect light differently, and brought depth to the all-white surround with architecturally detailed ceilings, paneled walls, and doors. By day (left), sunlight and views dominate, with the sparest possible mix of accessories and accents to distract from the view. At night (opposite), subtle washes of light from concealed lighting combine with judiciously placed lamps and shaded sconces to cast a flattering peachy glow.

No matter how desirable it is to let light into the home, it can be equally important to keep it out, or at least moderate its presence. Fade-sensitive colors and fabrics should not be used in sunlight-rich rooms (watch for this detail when you're shopping; blues tend to be the most susceptible). Delicate carpets and upholstery may need protection from direct sunlight, and even artificial light can be hazardous to artworks—museums rotate exhibits of photographs, works on paper and textiles to limit their exposure, even under low illumination.

In this antiques-and-art-filled Charleston, South Carolina, interior designed by Amelia T. Handegan, incoming light is diffused through softly shirred Roman blinds. Artificial light from antique fixtures is kept appropriately soft.

SCREENINGS

In his Arizona desert home, architect Jack DeBartolo Jr. created what is essentially a single large room (two views on these pages) backed by an entire wall of glass. A screening wall on the west side of the house (opposite) deflects the most intense desert heat, and the window walls slide open for natural ventilation. Sensibly shaded to moderate the strongest rays of the sun, the gently arching roof creates the effect of a spacious pavilion. Partitions running the length of the ceiling delineate living areas, which are furnished with bold contemporary pieces placed symmetrically on the bleached wood floor. Keeping things simple directs the focus to the panoramic views. To preserve the clean-lined architectural silhouette, lighting is entirely built in—a combination of tracks, recessed ceiling lights, and focused downlights on buffet, dining table, and a bold modern canvas (right).

As natural light flows from the outside in, artificial light can do the opposite. In the hours between dusk and dawn (or at least until bedtime), light can flow through wide-windowed spaces to illuminate outdoor areas and turn them into extensions of the home.

In this southern California house designed by architect Buzz Yudell, the transition between indoors and out has been almost entirely erased. Every room opens onto its own terrace, and a fireplace on the patio turns the house virtually inside-out on pleasant evenings, when sitting under the stars replaces sitting under the roof. Designer Audrey Alberts furnished the outdoor living room with comfortable seating and fabrics in a neutral palette that are treated for outdoor exposure. Plenty of light flows through the tall windows surrounding the space, and wall-mounted floods, together with firelight and candles, set a more romantic scene when the indoor lights are turned off.

Just because outdoor spaces have lots of natural light doesn't mean they won't benefit from some technological help. Architect Jack McCartney reclaimed the backyard of a Washington, D.C., house (left) with a three-story addition that created a new outdoor living space. A wide expanse of windows on two sides provides a view of the interiors. The outdoor lighting is hidden under the eaves of the roof. Opposite: Designer T. Keller Donovan carried the freshness of the mostly white color scheme in a rural Connecticut house onto a terrace lit only with candles. Safely contained and draft-resistant in white metal lanterns lined up along the balustrade, they're aided by light from inside the house. With clusters of candles on the table and the support of a moonlit night, they set a lovely scene.

When windows are left bare to let in natural light and allow full view of the scenery, they can be difficult to deal with after dark. Even in apartments with views of city skylines, looking out at night is often hampered by the indoor light, which throws glare on the glass, obscures the view, and can create an unpleasant expanse of blackness on window walls.

This Arizona house, designed by John Chonka for an art collector, has extraordinary views, and equally extraordinary treasures throughout its rooms. In the master bedroom and adjacent study, walls of aluminum-framed windows open onto a patio. By day, window shades of varying opacity help modulate the strong sunlight, which is more than enough to light the space. At night, downlights in the ceiling and strips under the custom white mahogany shelving illuminate the artworks and bathe the rooms in warm light.

Water is a reflective surface, which explains why pools and oceans take on the blue tints of the sky. Watertight lights beneath the rim of the pool can frame its outline, avoiding the unattractive look—and the potential hazard—of an invisible black hole. Poolside, electric outlets and fixtures should be out of splashing range. Permanent fixtures throwing soft overall light are most often mounted on an exterior building wall or on decorative posts.

In Brian Murphy's redesign of a midcentury Hollywood Hills home, the curves of the kidney-shaped vintage pool are echoed in the curving rear wall of the two-story living room (left). The area is well lit from within the house, and without. Opposite: For a more traditional look in her Sagoponack, New York, home, Nannette Brown has a clean-lined rectangular pool that balances the modern Palladian window of her double-height living room. The pool and adjoining courtyard are the focal point for summer entertaining, lit by under-eaves downlights and lots of paper-bag luminaries. (Party-pretty but not entirely practical, they're inexpensive enough to replace after every special-event use.)

The perfect home, in terms of lighting, is the one that's absolutely faultless, every hour of the day or night, in design impact and illumination efficiency. Such a place is rare, and almost always requires starting from scratch. The first challenge is to find the perfect location, with ideal natural light. The next is to site the house to capitalize on nature's benefits. The last, but far from least, is to design a lighting plan that first supplements natural light without upstaging it, then takes over after dark to create an experience that's as spectacular as the daylight-flooded one.

Architect Ken Shuttleworth's Crescent House in Wiltshire, England, is a superb example of just

all day all night

By day, light fills the large open living area, with its spare furnishings and wall of cubbyholes filled with a colorful collection of children's toys and artwork. Walls and ceiling are the brightest possible white, as is most of the furniture. All of the lighting is cleverly built in, allowing illumination to glow down from the ceiling without disturbing the flow of the space.

such a challenge well met. Translating the traditional English country house into an altogether modern vernacular, the innovative, comma-shaped structure he designed for his family was carefully oriented for natural warming and cooling, meeting the design challenge of environmental sensitivity as well as budgetary considerations. Its monolithic concrete entrance facade deflects the elements, acting as protection from wind and rain; the opposite side is a wall of glass that brings the outdoors and the daylight into every part of the house. The overwhelming feeling is an exhilarating one of openness, one that is carried out in the spare design of the rooms. The interior incorporates kitchen, living, dining, and playroom areas in one unbroken expanse,

Off the main area (above), a curved wall displays drawings by the homeowners' children. Concealed lighting reflects off white walls and soft gray carpeting. At night, the children's artwork is reflected in the windows (opposite), creating another wall of art.

Overleaf: The interior of the crescent opens onto a 300-foot-wide circular lawn, mowed in circles to reflect the shape of the house.

with stark white walls and ceiling that maximize both light and spaciousness. Furnishings are sparse, in simple black and white, but gain plenty of colorful sparkle from the children's toys and artwork, displayed as design elements as well as family treasures. A concrete fireplace is another warming touch. Though wildly innovative, the house is eminently practical, with a use of natural and artificial light that makes it a pleasure to look at, and to live in, at any hour of any season.

LIGH

Every lighting plan begins with the question: What type of space is being lit? The lighting needs of an entry foyer are very different from the needs of a kitchen or bath. The next question is: When will the space be used? Natural light shifts dramatically over the course of the day. Louvers, blinds, shades, and

the science of
TING

Brass spotlights, mounted on the
upper moldings of custom shelving,
cast just enough light to illuminate
book titles in the library of a
New York apartment (above).
Opposite: Built-in downlights heighten
the contrast between the white
elements and dark walls. A brass
picture light spotlights the oil painting.

solar screens can enhance and manipulate it; widening windows, adding new ones, or installing skylights are often worth the effort and expense. Moreover, lighting is not an independent element: it plays off other objects, so the contents of a room—major seating areas, art collections—should also be taken into consideration.

Artificial lighting must be flexible to accommodate variations in natural light. In selecting fixtures, decide which areas must be lit and which can stay in shadow; what furnishings to flatter, architectural elements to highlight, colors to complement. Then choose your weapons from four basic categories: ambient or overall light, task lighting for close work, indirect lighting, and decorative fixtures. The most frequently used types of lights—incandescent, halogen, and fluorescent—are available in all these categories, in different forms, intensities, and colorations. There are tabletop and standing lamps, chandeliers, pendants, and other suspension fixtures. There are globes, tracks, recessed cans, eyeballs, uplights and downlights, floods and spots, task lights, and concealed lighting elements, to name just a few.

Nothing is quite as dramatic as a chandelier, but it's more often a statement of good design than good lighting and must often be augmented by functional lighting. Its scale is as important as its style—it should neither overwhelm a space nor get lost in it. Hanging fixtures should clear the head of at least an average-size person yet be low enough to permit cleaning and changing bulbs. Dining fixtures are generally set at eighteen inches above the table.

Today, even tiny lamps can give off lots of illumination, so you can have light wherever you want it. For reading or desk work, choices range from the conventional incandescent shaded lamp to high-intensity, articulated worklights that adjust to the individual reader's height and posture, all available in wall-mounted, tabletop, standing, and clip-on versions. Though mostly modern in design, they are unobtrusive enough to fit into almost any interior.

The most efficient and economical lighting plans use both overall and directed lighting. Ambient light illuminates an entire space, but may be too much, or insufficiently focused, for close work. When light is directed toward a specific surface, less energy is needed to achieve the desired illumination. Translucent shades or frosted glass enclosures diffuse light, while opaque shades help to concentrate it. Built-in lighting can be diffused under coverings or reflected off walls and ceilings. Except for special types of decorative bare bulbs, lighting sources should not be entirely exposed: Looking into a light source, even a relatively dim one, is both uncomfortable and potentially harmful to the eyes.

The last step in developing a lighting plan is to judge just how much light a room needs. It's not an easy call. In general, the greater the volume of space, the greater the amount of light required, though factors such as the presence of reflective surfaces and the choice of colors in the room affects the equation. Lighting engineers determine it with scientific calculations, but an easy rule of thumb is that a room is well lit when the space feels comfortable.

In a bathroom with conversation-piece fittings (opposite), light issues from a simple frosted-globe fixture mounted over a spectacularly sculptured mirror. Above: A pair of slender metal-and-glass lamps flanks a tall mirror over the dresser in fashion designer Adrienne Vittadini's bedroom. The dove-gray walls in its reflection set off old master etchings.

Where built-in lighting is too costly or not feasible, tiny fixtures can make themselves scarce. In the library nook of architect Alison Spear's whitewashed Miami apartment (right), a skinny metal light is mounted over the bookshelves, where it's barely noticeable. Opposite left: In a dining room alcove, recessed cans shed light on artwork and the serving sink below. Opposite right: Peter Shelton and Lee Mindel made the lighting a part of the architecture in a minimalist New York residence, where polished white walls float on white-lacquered floors, reflecting the diffused glow from the frosted-glass ceiling panel.

The architecturally innovative home on these pages showcases a major collection of West Virginia art and crafts. To set it off, architect Laura Hartman created a series of shedlike structures around a grassy courtyard. The flowing, well-windowed expanses of the interconnected rooms offer solitude as well as space for entertaining. In parts of the multilevel structure, additional light streams in from second-story windows. In the main living space, one wall is used as a picture gallery, while corners make effective display areas for three-dimensional art. Running like a spine along the length of the space, track lighting becomes a design element as well as a means of illumination. Individual fixtures can be moved to focus wherever they're needed, according to the time of day or to changes in the displays of art. Polished wood floors throughout the space anchor the furnishings.

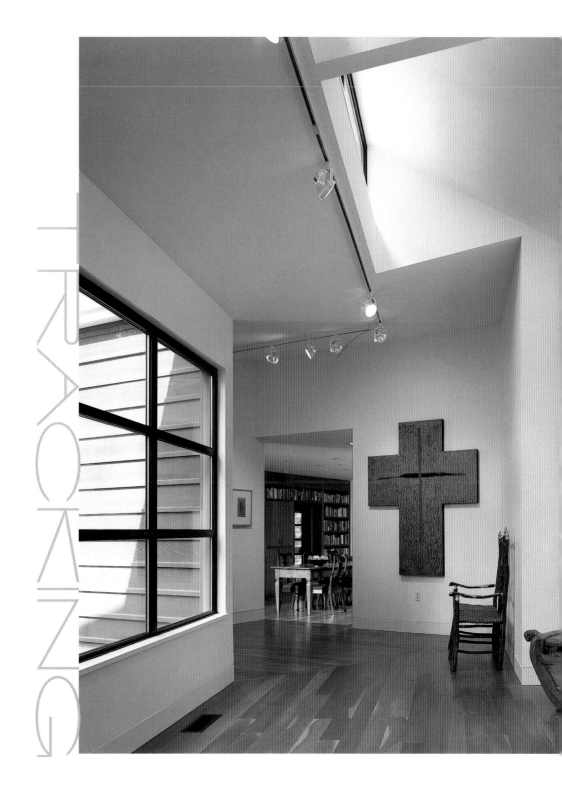

Art under glass can't tolerate glare, while dark-toned oils may need more than the usual intensity of light. Shadows must be manipulated to properly set off three-dimensional works; and textiles, which fade easily, must be protected from too much exposure to light. In other words, no single solution works for every kind of art.

In a 1920s Washington, D.C., home (opposite), the renovated living room is cleanly modern. A wall-to-wall arrangement of photos and works on paper, all in identical white mats and silvery-tone frames, hangs over bookshelves topped by family pictures. Illuminating it all is a row of lights recessed into the ceiling and half shaded to focus on the showcase wall. For reading, simple brass standing lamps flank the sofas. Left: In a Manhattan loft designed by Hugh Newell Jacobsen, most of the windows are on the perimeter, leaving a windowless hallway in the center. The architect turned it into a functioning art gallery, with a row of track lighting to dramatize its length and illuminate a series of oil paintings. Flanking the track, air-conditioning slits look like architectural accents.

special-purpose lighting

Lighting a room doesn't always finish the job. The difference between just-okay and just-what-you-need are the extra little details.

Kitchens need light for three specific tasks: choosing food (refrigerators have interior lights, but many cabinet interiors could use lighting, too), preparing food (over the cooktop and major work surfaces), and cleaning up (over the sink). Fluorescent strips were once the under-cabinet norm, but halogen lighting now offers many more variations in size, color, and design. Full-spectrum lighting is best over food-preparation areas; it renders colors with maximum accuracy, allowing you to see whether foods are fresh.

Bedside lamps are usually decorative and rarely provide adequate reading light. Wall-mounted lamps, adjustable for sitting-up or reclining-in-bed reading, are a much better choice. They're available in both incandescent and halogen versions, and in styles that are compatible with traditional or contemporary design schemes. Fixtures with extension arms and a broad light spread can accommodate those who like to work in bed.

Bathrooms are seldom adequately lit. Most require lighting in three areas: overall (overhead), on either side of the mirror, and over the bathtub or the shower. Lighting for grooming and makeup should be directed onto the face from both sides to avoid casting unflattering shadows. A small plug-in safety light is an added convenience.

Closets are among the most useful places to install lights. Even a simple frosted bulb can help illuminate dark corners. If an electric outlet isn't available, an easy-to-install, inexpensive battery-powered fixture will do the trick.

Art is a particular challenge. The entire surface of paintings or framed works should be lit evenly, without glare, with colors rendered accurately, and with a minimum of heat and ultraviolet or infrared rays. To light art effectively without damaging it, picture lights with long arms that direct light evenly onto the painting, and color-correct, ultraviolet-free, low-wattage bulbs, can be mounted on the back of a frame. Fiber-optic lights are free of damaging ultraviolet and infrared rays, but they're expensive to install. These and other custom lighting options are best left to specialists. Sculptures, often less sensitive than framed art, should be lit to enhance their forms, and sometimes to cast shadows. There are uplights and downlights of various sizes and configurations designed to do the job for any particular piece.

Bookshelves and display cabinets can often benefit from special lighting. Lights designed to clip onto shelves or mount beneath them are available.

Safety on stairs—indoors, at entrances, on porches and patios—is more important than aesthetics. Outdoor areas, especially near ponds or swimming pools, should be well lit. Dim, shadowy lighting makes for dangerous missteps and accidents.

Book-filled shelves tend to
absorb light, making rooms seem
darker. Adding ambient lighting
is one solution; painting shelves
 white and choosing pale-toned
furnishings is another.

　　In an inviting New York
apartment, designer Benjamin
Noriega-Ortiz placed bracket-mounted
shaded lamps on the uprights of the
built-in bookcase; there they provide
both illumination and decorative
accent. To avoid the dark, heavy look
that bookshelves can give a modest-
size room, he kept these high and
uncluttered, filling the recesses below
with white-matted photographs.
Pale upholstery, bleached-wood tables,
and off-white carpeting maximize
the light and openness of the space.

Few home decorating schemes take well to the functional fixtures used in most commercial spaces. What's needed are fixtures that combine efficient lighting for the desktop with attractive design, regardless of the style. A chrome-and-glass desk (left), is lit by a modern metal swing-arm lamp that suits it well for both style and illumination. Opposite: When designer Mark Hampton placed a fine English Georgian desk and chair in front of a massive Dutch leather screen, it needed light that wouldn't spoil the elegant composition. His choice: a pair of simple all-brass lamps whose light is focused down onto the desktop.

A black metal-and-chrome clip-on lamp, clamped onto built-in bookshelves (opposite), pairs well with Breuer tables and crisp white linen upholstery in a weekend house designed by Monte Coleman. Top right: Designer Christian Liaigre placed a skinny standing lamp in just the right spot—close enough to the comfortable lounge chair, and low enough to avoid blocking the pictures on the wall behind it. Bottom right: In designer David Hicks's London apartment, a flamboyant William Kent–designed eagle table upstages everything around it. A thin standing brass lamp modestly avoids interference, yet provides fine light for reading.

GOOD READING

Over-the-dining-table lighting is often more concerned with providing atmosphere than illumination. In formal dining rooms especially, the main objective is usually to flatter the diners—hence the popularity of candlelight. On the other hand, most of us like to be able to see what we are eating. A delicate compromise is called for.

Top left: In a French country–style dining room with a wood-beamed ceiling and a collection of Delft on display, an antique lantern, electrified and fitted with candelabra bulbs, satisfies both function and style. Bottom left: Suzanne Rheinstein's "ultimate party kitchen" is mainly used for professional food preparation. A simple globe fixture, out of the way of the busy working staff, provides the required overhead light for informal in-kitchen meals. Opposite: In a Long Island weekend house designed by Vicente Wolf, light floods in through a wall of windows facing the sea. After sundown, the inviting dining area is illuminated by a broad, silk-shaded incandescent fixture, its flattering glow complemented by candles.

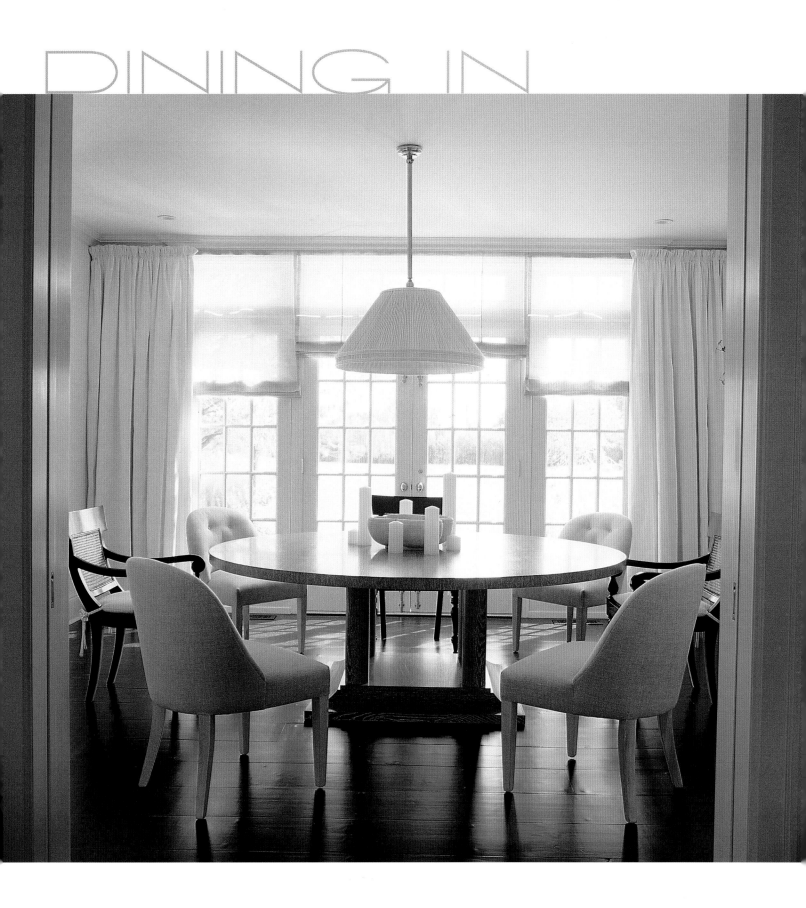

A generous helping of bright red is just the ticket for a room that's not quite light enough or one that may be too brightly lit. From persimmon to cherry, burgundy to lipstick bright, there's probably no single color that elicits such enthusiasm. In rooms with natural lighting, the contrast of red and white is almost always a winner, mixing hot and cold in just the right proportions. Designer Libby Cameron, furnishing a house in Maine for red-loving clients, picked a rich, lacquery tone for the dining room walls, then surrounded it with the freshness of white on moldings, furniture, and textured sisal carpet. Printed chintz curtains frame the view, and sheer white casements beneath help to mute the glare of all-day sun. An antique painted tole chandelier lights up the dining table.

Richard Sapper designed the Tizio lamp in 1970. More than thirty years later, its bold modern lines have made it a classic. Top left: The lamp comfortably fits in with a quirky mix of styles in a neoclassical sitting room. Bottom left: Bulky lamps would be out of place in the pale-toned living room of designer Albert Hadley's Florida cottage, a smallish space clothed in white and gray paint and pale-toned upholstery. A pair of cantilever-arm metal standing lamps, alongside skirted high-back chairs, facilitates fireside reading. Opposite: A 25-foot-square marble-topped worktable, a treasured object in the Greenwich Village duplex of photographer Oberto Gili and stylist Wendy Goodman, is perfect for rolling out pasta as well as for dining. Two swing-arm lamps have weighty bases that allow them to dip low enough to light intricate food-preparation tasks. For dining, they're easily removed.

BALANCING ACT

The most romantic artificial light, though not necessarily the most efficient, comes from the flattering glow of candles. Modern candelabra bulbs produce look-alike flickers of light without the inconvenience of draft-susceptible flutters or wax drippings on the table. Fine reproduction fixtures emulate the look of candled chandeliers. Old pieces can be electrified, with one note of caution: Such alteration will probably decrease the value of a fine antique, requiring a choice between convenience and investment potential.

Opposite: In fashion designer Adrienne Vittadini's classically furnished New York apartment, dining is by the candlelight of an extravagant crystal chandelier. Right: A candle-fitted tole-and-brass chandelier is suspended by a tasseled cord from the high beamed ceiling of Paul Wiseman's San Francisco apartment. More candles, in a circlet of silver candlesticks, dress the oval table beneath. The English Regency design of the fixture complements the neoclassical furnishings and framed cabinetmaker's engravings. To suggest endless space beyond and to double the lighting effect, the designer fixed a pair of mirror-paneled doors to the back wall.

GOLDEN GLOW

For her beachhouse getaway on Long Island, Los Angeles designer Kelly Harmon moved a nineteenth-century farmhouse to the dunes. Then she added new wings, made with old materials that make them almost indistinguishable from the original space. Recycled wood beams, plastered walls, and mostly Swedish antiques carry out the cozy country mood. The only visible lighting comes from Belgian beeswax candles, the designer's choice for their flattering light and soft golden color. All the other lighting is low and camouflaged. Left: In a corner of the kitchen, complete with original wood beams, is a tiny Swedish tin chandelier, more useful for its whimsical charm than its illumination power. Opposite: Natural daylight from French doors and a clerestory window warms the dining room's Old World antiques. In the evening, candle glow comes from an iron-and-glass chandelier with unusual bud-vase fittings that hold wildflowers interspersed among the candles. On the walls are shaded candles in iron-and-horn antique sconces.

This California kitchen designed by Fu-Tung Cheng is a masterpiece of wood, concrete, and metal, with an angular beamed ceiling and roof-high windows that admit light without breaking up the flow of the two-story space. Spanning the lofty room, adjustable low-voltage lighting is mounted on horizontal steel cables, while brushed-steel pendants spotlight the center island. The steel stove hood has its own built-in lighting element, and undercabinet fluorescents illuminate each work area. The overall look of Zen-like serenity belies the buttoned-up efficiency of this well-conceived and well-equipped space.

COOKING LIGHT

For kitchens that lean more toward country classic than twenty-first-century chic, it's possible to find authentic old fixtures or up-to-date fixtures styled with an eye to tradition.

Top left: A well-equipped kitchen combines modern convenience with a touch of traditional style—classic stove, country furnishings, and shelves of country crockery. Old-style but newly made painted aluminum pendant fixtures light the workspace without disrupting the mood. Bottom left: Old and new team up in a southern California kitchen designed by Rob Wellington Quigley. Heat-resistant, double-layered glass makes large expanses of window practical in the oceanfront location, letting in daylight and cross-ventilation. The industrial-style track lighting is practical and unobtrusive, and the sleek steel countertops are warmed by wood cabinetry and terra-cotta walls. Opposite: Modern with an ethereal Eastern accent, a New York loft kitchen area uses shoji-like glass panels to form a counterpoint to hard-edged wood and stone. Over the work island architects Antonio Morello and Donato Savoie used adjustable high-intensity fixtures, so simple, tiny, and white that they virtually disappear from sight.

In a San Francisco kitchen (right), a polished-steel range hood tops a professional-quality stove. Bright lights behind the hood fan out to serve the adjacent countertops as well. Opposite left: In a modern apartment building where exterior venting isn't possible, a built-in circulating fan, with its own fluorescent light element focused on the stovetop, takes the place of a range hood. Opposite right: Architect John Chonka's down-focused spot lighting, installed under a cabinet in a modern Arizona kitchen, are like streaks of sunlight playing on the counter below.

For relaxing and reading, or even working in bed, lighting is generally mounted on the wall behind the bed or placed on adjacent night tables. Too often, however, wall lights are set too far to the side, and table lamps cast light mostly on the tables themselves, requiring awkward bending or tilting shades to illuminate reading matter, paper, or a laptop screen. Adjustable wall-mounted, high-intensity lights are the most practical, and most efficient, solution.

In the bedroom of a generously windowed West Virginia home (left), lighting for the country-style iron beds is provided by simple polished-aluminum gooseneck lamps on the dresser between them. Opposite top: Designer Todd Klein used wall-mounted lamps with broad parchment shades in the bedroom of a Louisville house. They spread the light enough to allow for reading comfort, and they suit the Deco-style furnishings. Opposite bottom: Designer Michael Formica avoided competing with the shapely headboard of a vintage Vladimir Kagan bed by choosing a pair of super-skinny floor lamps.

DRESSING UP

At the dressing table, the color of light is just as critical as the quantity. Clear, full-spectrum light is called for in daylight, while evening lights may have a pink or golden tone. The best solution is a professional-caliber makeup mirror with self-contained lighting designed to register skin tones with maximum accuracy.

In a gentleman's bedroom designed by Brian Killian (opposite), where warm-toned mahogany is accented with steel, aluminum, and pewter, halogen downlights are well suited to the desk–dressing table alcove. On the desk is a pair of stainless-steel-and-ebony lamps with frosted glass shades. Right: The mostly white dressing area in the 1835 guesthouse of a South Carolina plantation boasts a straightforward pair of silk-shaded glass lamps that suit the old-fashioned style of the skirted dressing table.

No cold fluorescents or high-intensity tungsten-halogen lights are welcome in the bathroom— just good, clear-white, even illumination. For the mirror, soft light from above or the sides is best—light that doesn't create unflattering shadows.

Opposite: Thomas O'Brien designed a Manhattan bathroom– sitting room with retro-style glamour. The 600-square-foot space, with white walls, white tile, and marble mosaics, takes the chill off with warm wood accents. There's plenty of natural light from windows and a skylight, and tall mirrors to reflect it. Clean-lined steel-framed incandescents flank the mirrors. Top right: A standard New York apartment bathroom was updated by Ken Foreman with a sliding wall that opens to the bedroom, turning the space into a suite. Furnished in pale boudoir tones, it's fitted with recessed ceiling downlights that are reflected in the mirror and shower door and continue into the bedroom beyond. Bottom right: In the double-shower enclosure of a Southern California bathroom by architect Buzz Yudell, a pair of wall-mounted frosted hemispheres provide light for showering under ceiling-mounted sprays.

a lighting primer

Incandescent light, the most familiar and popular form of indoor lighting, is also the oldest. It is basically the same as the 40-hour bulb patented in 1879 by Thomas Edison: a thin filament wire in a vacuum within a sealed glass container on a screw-in metal base. When electric current is passed through the wire, it becomes white-hot and generates light. Today's version, made with tungsten filaments, is available in clear or frosted, in a mind-boggling range of shapes, sizes, variations, and tints. Incandescent light generally has a warm yellowish cast.

Fluorescent light, invented in 1938, produces illumination by a combination of glowing gas and fluorescent phosphors. A sealed bulb, usually tubular, is filled with mercury vapor and its interior coated with phosphors. When electric current passes through, the gas produces ultraviolet radiation, which in turn acts on the phosphors to emit light. Fluorescent bulbs illuminate gradually, and their light fades with age. Because it uses far less electricity than incandescent light; lasts as much as twenty times longer; and produces an even, diffuse light, fluorescent lighting is the form most commonly used in commercial interiors. Its drawback is its skewed color, a cold, bluish white, although improved versions more closely duplicate the quality of incandescent or natural light. In the home, fluorescent lighting is most often used in kitchens and undercabinet fixtures.

Halogen lighting, more accurately called tungsten-halogen, is a variant of incandescent lighting. Halogen gases such as iodine or bromine added to the bulb allow a higher filament temperature. The reaction between tungsten and halogen increases the life of the bulb to an average of 4,000 hours by returning evaporated particles to the filament. Low-voltage halogens have a smaller filament, enabling use of a smaller bulb, which provides a concentrated, controllable light source; a transformer, usually built into the fixture, steps down the wattage. Standard-voltage halogens avoid the added weight and cost of a transformer, but they are generally larger. Their pin base sits more sturdily in the socket than the screw-in variety. Introduced as reading lights, halogen fixtures are also used for spotlights, reflectors, and specialized accent lighting. Their primary drawback is the intense heat, which can cause burns, even fires. Halogens need protective housing and should always be placed where nothing can touch them. The bulb surface should never be touched, as skin oils dissipate the life of the lamp. Their bright, white light is closest to the color of direct sunlight.

Other lighting: Mercury vapor, high-pressure sodium, and neon lights are available on the market. Most have specific commercial applications and are seldom used in the home.

An extra row of molding-high windows punctuates the stratospheric height of an airy living room, opposite. French doors on two walls open to let in daylight and views, and the patio roof serves as a shield against midday glare. Romantic, functional suspended ceiling fans have built-in lights for overall evening glow.

Top left: In a lofty Florida living-dining room designed by William Diamond and Anthony Baratta, the palest buttery yellow walls, cooled by classical white molding and perky pastel print fabrics, makes the most of daylight streaming through five pairs of tall French doors and an oval window punched into the space above. Tall broad-shaded table lamps match the superscale seating. An old iron hanging lantern is more for atmosphere than function. Bottom left: The double-height entry in the same house is a symphony of garden hues, with light flowing in through high windows. Yellow-green walls create a sunny mood on even the grayest days, and the glow of incandescent lighting—hanging lantern and shaded girandoles on the walls—re-creates it at night.

S ome of the best-lit interiors are illuminated entirely from invisible sources, where light itself, rather than lighting elements, becomes part of the architecture. This kind of treatment is customary in dramatic modern spaces, where lamps and sconces would interrupt the clean linearity.

Opposite: A kitchen–living room–great room in California's woodsy Marin County features built-in recessed lighting that illuminates the room to high-tech perfection. Several types of lighting—incandescent, fluorescent, and halogen—provide the appropriate quality and quantity of light for each area. Designer Fu-Tung Cheng crafted the space in sleek modern materials—pale woods, concrete, polished stone, and steel. But the simplicity is deceptive: The asymmetrical cabinets and the off-angled center-island counter, with its steel shelf and built-in maple cutting board, are all intricately detailed. A single graceful Tizio lamp augments the seating-area lighting. Right: In designer Christian Liaigre's nineteenth-century Paris house, a luxurious, understated, skylit dressing room is wrapped in oak cupboards outfitted with all the accoutrements of the well-dressed gentleman. At night, concealed lighting kicks in.

It's easy to understand why so many homes skimp on lighting. Instead of being worked out in advance, it's often thought of at the end of the project—when most of the funds have already been spent—so many people settle for what they can get. They assume that custom lighting will be too costly, and usually don't even bother to consult a designer or lighting specialist. The home profiled here was built on a very strict budget, with a lighting plan to match, but there's no look of penny-pinching about either house or illumination. Granted, it took considerable time and effort, and the owners are themselves architects, but their enterprising ideas are a testament to the possibility of

light touch

do-it-yourself ingenuity and resourceful planning.

Peter McMahon and Susan Jennings built their light-filled Cape Cod vacation home over six summers, doing the work themselves, with the help of friends. The vacation house, built almost entirely from salvaged materials, is a light-saturated, aluminum-roofed space with a curving, 13-foot-high ceiling and an entire wall of glass. Fixed plate glass panels reach for every possible ray of daylight, and a high clerestory window brings in the sunset as well. All this openness makes the house look much larger than its 650 square feet. For this type of interior, the conventional choice would have been track or recessed lighting—very effective but relatively costly options. Instead, the

In the main living area of this budget-minded beach house, the high, curved ceiling is paneled in pine, but the flooring and cabinets are ordinary plywood. Floodlights across the tops of the cabinetry are focused upward for reflected light. In the kitchen, the floods are flipped to serve as downlights for the work areas.

The plywood platform bed and simple bookcases in the master bedroom (above) keep things clean and simple. Lighting means windows by day and functional floodlights by night. Opposite: A built-in seating platform in the living room is prettied up with lots of pillows and a casual combination of yard-sale furnishings and pieces built by McMahon, such as the plywood chair. Lively color makes the sparkling setting even more appealing.

owners installed ordinary exterior floodlights, which did the job for a fraction of the price, and without sacrificing a drop of style. For everything else, working on a budget meant using inexpensive materials and buying furniture at flea markets and yard sales. The result, though unpretentious, is certainly long on style. And for a total cost that stayed well within their ultra-conservative budget, the couple's hard work obviously paid off.

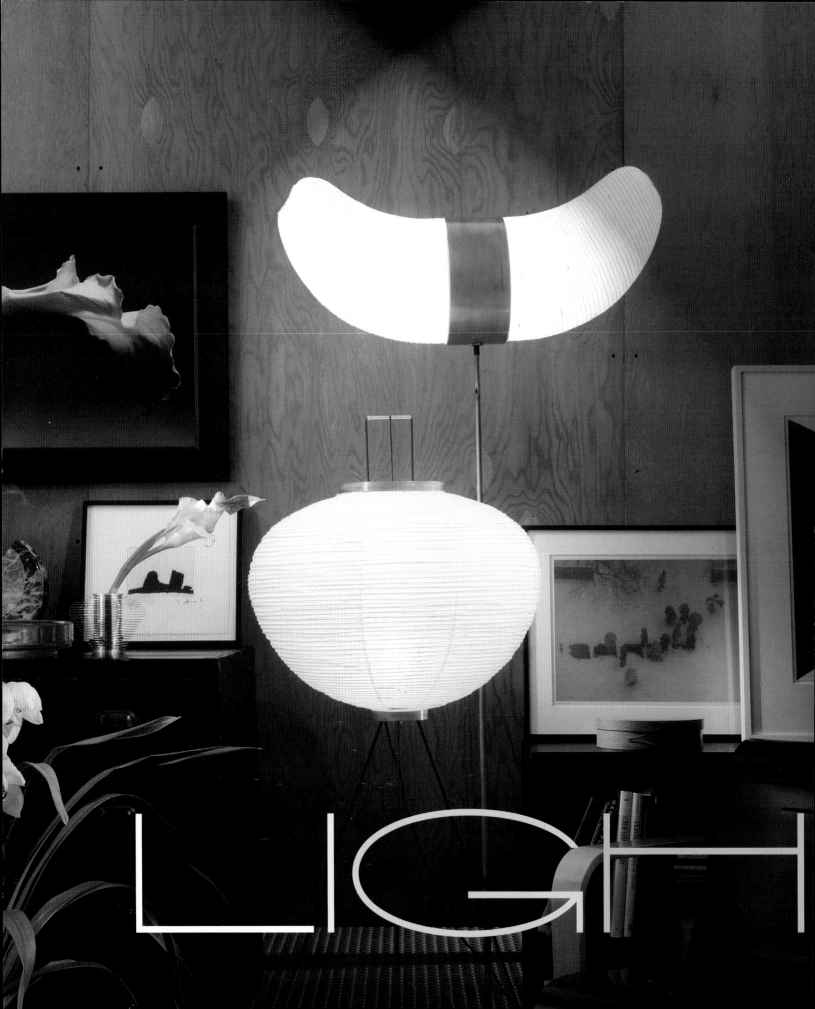

LIGH

Brilliance, gleam, luster, sparkle . . . these are some of the evocative words in the enchanting language of light. Artful lighting is as essential to a beautiful interior as its most prominent piece of furniture or finest work of art. Filling space without intruding upon it, light meshes with the architecture to dramatize focal

the **art** of TING

In a cozy weekend home (above), a collector with a penchant for bee objects casts soft light on some of her treasures with a beehive-shaped lamp and a silk shade with the same silhouette. Opposite: A Turkish lantern serves as art rather than illumination in a decorative tablescape in designer Vicente Wolf's New York apartment.

points and minimize awkward proportions, casting shadows that define beautiful objects as they mask details best left unnoticed. It transforms a mere assemblage of furnishings into a harmonious whole. In so doing, lighting orchestrates a design with instruments that are, if not precisely works of art, then surely artful devices.

Windows, the first avenues of light, do more than simply transmit it—they can filter or color it or add other qualities. Glass is an infinitely flexible material that can be molded, frosted, etched, or sculpted by modern glass artists drawing inspiration from traditional masterpieces—the stained glass of medieval cathedrals, Tiffany's favrile-glass pictorials, or the modern "light screens" of Frank Lloyd Wright—to create windows that serve as major design elements without abandoning their light-giving roles.

The instruments of artificial lighting can be as creatively varied as any other works of art. The most dramatic are chandeliers, which bring instant glamour to any room by evoking the splendor of elegant mansions or manor halls. Cut crystal is the most common material, but there are many other options: brass, wrought iron, tole, even ceramic or wood. They may be fine antiques or authentic reproductions, in classical, colonial, country, or contemporary styles. Ultramodern interiors can find their match in chandeliers of steel, chrome, plastic, even paper—think of Poul Henningsen's copper Artichoke, George Nelson's sprayed-plastic Bubble lamp, or Isamu Noguchi's paper Akari lanterns.

There are as many lamps in today's design world as there are rooms in which to place them. Alternatively, a lamp can be improvised from other objects—ceramics, sculptures, vases, or pitchers—making individualistic design statements of their own. Lamps can also be works of art themselves; witness the sculptural creations of Italian designers such as Achille Castiglioni and Joe Columbo, or the idiosyncratic glass lights hand blown by American craftsman Dale Chihuly. These, and their like, can be placed in a room as precisely as paintings or sculptures, with equally flattering results.

Lighting that is built into the architecture, and largely concealed by it, is artful in a different way: Here, light itself becomes the evanescent and constantly changing design element. It can be deployed in shadings of intensity, color, and emphasis to create a particular mood—the liveliness of a bright room, the intimacy of a softly lit one, or any number of sophisticated variations. In an art-filled living room, for example, the interplay of light and shadow can highlight important works and downplay lesser ones. Candles and subtle downlight on a dining room table flatter the guests and illuminate the food, while dimness in the surrounding space enhances the feeling of intimacy. Similarly, soft light focused on a comfortable seating area encourages cozy groupings and intimate conversation. When the same room hosts a large gathering, bright light distributed evenly throughout the space fosters a flow of movement and lively talk. And in homes endowed with a porch or patio, exterior lighting adds drama and facilitates outdoor get-togethers.

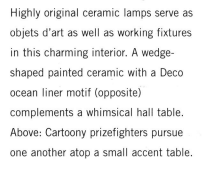

Highly original ceramic lamps serve as objets d'art as well as working fixtures in this charming interior. A wedge-shaped painted ceramic with a Deco ocean liner motif (opposite) complements a whimsical hall table. Above: Cartoony prizefighters pursue one another atop a small accent table.

An exuberant antique Venetian glass chandelier lends a glamorous touch to architect Alison Spear's neomodernist all-white Miami apartment (top left). In Paola Navone's converted-warehouse duplex in Milan (bottom left), a votive-candle metal-and-glass chandelier adds color and a strong note of whimsy to soften the look of a high-tech iron staircase. Opposite: A Murano masterpiece, more than five feet tall, was custom-designed for the high-ceilinged space and six-foot dining table in Hugh and Tiziana Hardy's New York loft. The extravagant design, inspired by one the homeowners had admired in a museum, has an added attraction— the floral ornaments on the upper levels can be changed with the season (here, blue for winter). To enhance the glow, the white stucco walls have been rubbed with aluminum powder.

CHANDELIERS

Opposite: In a minuscule kitchen by Christopher Coleman (left), the window frames Dorothy Haffner's fused-glass artwork, flooding the space with color and masking an ugly view. Designer Jarrett Hedborg and artist George C. Scott conceived a winning starfish window (right) for a romantic accent in a Laguna Beach, California, cottage. Left: A traditional curved staircase paired with a geometric composition in leaded glass lends heightened drama to Patrice Gruffaz's Paris apartment.

Glass takes on a whole new personality when blown into colorful hanging fixtures that serve as ceiling-hung centerpieces for a table or a room. Some of the most ingenious of these began life as something else—a bowl, a sturdy jar, a set of stacking containers or whimsical candle-holders—while some are the inspired fantasies of contemporary craftsmen.

A sparkling blue covered-jar shape (opposite), minus the candle it originally held, stands up to the other furnishings in this fearlessly colorful Provençal farmhouse designed by Michel Klein and Joel Fournier. The giddy abundance of color—tangerine walls, purple door, multicolored kilim rug—needed grounding as well as light, and this pendant does the trick. In Ashley and Allegra Hicks's London house (right), the blue-and-white kitchen gets a pick-me-up red accent with an offbeat artwork-cum-chandelier. The double-globe design is surrounded by teardrops that dangle from space age–style antenna arms.

BRANCHING OUT

Chandeliers can take on the form of blown glass or metal trees, translucent or painted white, as airy and evanescent as the rays that stream through their intertwining branches. Something this spectacular in the way of lighting, especially in a relatively simple interior, is all the design interest a room can ask for. Two delightful examples enlighten this elegant home. The white-on-white living room (opposite) admits clear daylight through large, softly curtained windows. The filtered rays illuminate the weeping willow shape of a chandelier that looks every bit as pretty in daylight as it does lighted after dark. Twin translucent torchères fade almost to invisibility during the day. The airy ambience of the room is enhanced by the bare floor and spare furnishings. Left: Centered over an old-style cast-iron tub, the high-flying chandelier has the romantic look of snow-covered trees in a winter landscape—cool comfort for a steamy bath.

In a huge Connecticut barn
converted into an elegant country
house, a 30-by-40-foot living
room, whose walls open to the
surrounding landscape via a series of
large-as-possible modern windows,
takes center stage. Spectacular
lighting objects serve as art by day
and necessities by night, gently
illuminating treasures that range
from the classical to the not-quite
contemporary. Tiffany favrile
glass lamps are flanked by single
and multiple tulip lamps on
the tables. Functional modern brass
standing lamps provide practical
task light for reading, and an Edgar
Brandt Cobra torchère adds
flatttering soft uplight. The room's
overall illumination, though
relatively low, suits the old-fashioned
coziness of the space.

The sophistication of city living—especially in a penthouse aerie like this one—calls for lighting with particular panache. Challenged by the wraparound views of this Boston duplex for an art-collecting bachelor client, designer Celeste Cooper chose fixtures as bold and modern as the furnishings she used throughout the apartment. No glass or crystal here—the material of choice was polished steel, a fitting complement to the rich woods and mahogany paneling that wrap the soigné space. Opposite: An important bronzed-nickel and parchment fixture, 42 inches in diameter, hangs high over the dining table so as not to distract from the panoramic view outside. Looking toward the kitchen (right), the sinuous tentacles of a custom metal fixture suspended over the work-area countertop add a highly original sculptural accent. Fitted with tiny point lights, they serve as functional lighting for food preparation. Recessed ceiling spots keep the look sleek throughout the rest of the space.

Because the surface of a glossy white shade acts as a built-in reflector, radiating and intensifying the illumination, the choice of white fixtures is practical as well as aesthetic. In a spectacular showcase of a dining room (opposite), Orlando Diaz-Azcuy makes his boldest statement with a 9-foot marble table, modulating its massive scale with an oversize tray planted with a lawn of grass. How to top that? With an equally imposing cone-shape light that repeats the circular motif and is further echoed in the coffered ceiling. Walls, floors, and curtains in tones of muted grays soften the edginess of so much crisp geometry. Right: Master designer Vico Magistretti chose two bright white pendant lights for his own Milan apartment. Making a grand-scale statement in the kitchen (above) is a simple half-globe of enameled steel. It provides general lighting for the room, as well as focused work-area illumination. The skylight adds an atmospheric grace note. In the dining room (below), where the walls of the nineteenth-century building have been punched out to create wall-to-wall windows, a shapely pendant light of painted aluminum fits in with the airy mood created by the pure white walls and pale birch furnishings.

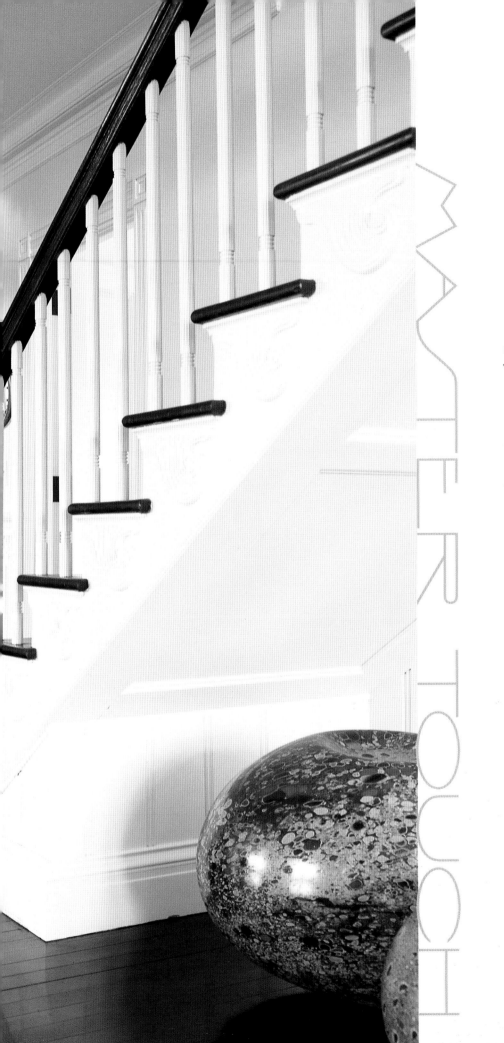

Some of today's glass craftsmen have broadened their horizons beyond bowls, vases, and drinking vessels, creating unique sculptures and lighting fixtures. Internationally celebrated Dale Chihuly, for example, has translated his hand-blown freeform floral sculptures into lighting designs that are functional works of art.

In this nineteenth-century shingle-style house on Long Island updated by Jed Johnson and Alan Wanzenberg, the light-reflecting glass of a Chihuly chandelier is the focal point in the entry hall. The artist's spatter-patterned freeform globe shapes sit comfortably beneath the staircase.

working with light

No matter how good it is in itself, light often needs a little help to do its job effectively and efficiently. Fortunately, its very intangibility makes it flexible to work with. Light can be spread or narrowed, angled, or muted. It can be played off its own natural tendencies by magnifying it against reflecting surfaces to brighten a space, or by diffusing and muting it to cut glare, underscore detail, and create an atmosphere of calm and intimacy.

Daylight can be made to travel farther, last longer, and glare less with the right window treatments. Even the simplest curtains will help diffuse brightness, and blinds and louvers will angle it. More sophisticated treatments such as vertical blinds and solar shades are available in dozens of materials that do everything from softly screening the light to blocking it entirely. After sundown, they can screen out the blackness of windows.

Mirrors have been used since the seventeenth century to help make interiors look larger and more resplendent. A mirror in the right place visually enlarges a room and doubles the effect of the light, natural or artificial, within. Before you hang a mirror, be sure it reflects something you want to see.

Polished surfaces, though not as dramatic as mirrors, also reflect light: Crystal chandeliers multiply the effectiveness of the bulbs they hold and may not need as much wattage as metal or wood ones to generate the same illumination. But reflections can be a problem as well as an advantage. In a room with many reflective objects—silver, brass, stainless steel, even lacquered and polished furniture—light focused directly on these surfaces may create distracting reflections and blur their details rather than enhancing them.

Finally, the surfaces of a room can be pressed into service as light reflectors. Ceilings are the most reflective and floors the least; walls fall between the two. White is obviously the most reflective, but a pale pastel has a similar effect. Fixtures that cast light over an entire pale wall or ceiling maximize its reflectivity. A white room not only appears lighter, but actually is so, while dark rooms need more illumination to be equally lit. High-gloss paints, as opposed to matte finishes, up the reflective quotient, but also show up every irregularity in a less-than-perfect surface.

Lampshades, in paper, silk, glass, or metal, can diffuse or direct light in specific amounts and directions. The basic shade has many variations: the degree of angle, from cylinder to parasol-wide, determines the spread of light both above and beneath it. Some are patterned or pierced, casting patterns of light on the walls and furnishings around them. Others have reflective interiors that redirect or intensify the light they contain.

Light can also be controlled with technical assistance. Easy-to-install dimmers adjust light to the level appropriate for any time of day or night, and are capable of working a bit of magic in just about every room in the house.

ver the past few decades, lamps designed by artists and architects have become as collectible as midcentury furniture. They serve as objects of both art and function and go a long way in enhancing an overall aesthetic statement. Often, the choice of such unique fixtures is dictated by the objects in an existing collection of furniture or art.

Left: In a composition of twentieth-century masterpieces arranged by architects Peter Stamberg and Paul Aferiat for a New York loft, two striking Isamu Noguchi standing lamps have no trouble holding their own alongside a black-stained Alvar Aalto chair and a Frank Gehry ottoman. Artful graphics are by Richard Serra and Ellsworth Kelly; the collage is by Robert Rauschenberg. Opposite: Designer Barbara Barry hung Ingo Maurer's grand "Floatation" ceiling fixture in a California entry foyer, then repeated its bold, circular form in a Roy Lichtenstein print. Anchoring the light tones is a pair of Mario Bellini leather chairs.

Standing lamps with long, thin arms may sometimes be awkward, but when properly chosen, they can be important decorative statements. Opposite: Michael Formica, a master of organizing space and an avid admirer of midcentury styles, designed a neutral-tone living room in a Long Island waterfront house around his clients' collection of 1940s and 1950s French furniture. Softly draped windows silhouette a Gio Ponti credenza and the exceptional elegance of a pair of standing wrought-metal lamps by Jean Royère. Curvy Vladimir Kagan sofas are comfortably oversize but subtle enough to avoid competing with the forms of the lamps or the Alexander Noll sculptures. Left: Gino Sarfatti's 1950s classic three-armed lamp takes its rightful place of honor as a sculptural presence in an apartment filled with fine modern furniture and graphics. It's practical, too—the arms can be repositioned and the metal shades tilt up or down as needed.

The provocative shapes of quirky lamps and chandeliers are emphasized by the illuminating rays of the lighting elements within them. Almost anything can be turned into lighting, from antique urns and teapots to hollow sculptures and shells. Some of the most attractive are entirely original.

In the dining room (originally a billiard room) of Larry Laslo's spacious New York apartment (opposite), the exuberant curves of a Tommi Parzinger mid-twentieth-century chandelier cast a spell. Light streams ceilingward and escapes in shapely rays from the punctured metal shades. A piece like this is just as attractive unlit as it is after dark. Right: Sandra Nunnerley designed a cozy dining corner illuminated by a wall-hung lamp made from hollowed-out coconut shells. Diffused light emerges gently from the sides. Looking like a string of suns, it serves equally well as a piece of sculpture.

Renzo Mongiardino designed an elegant foyer in a New York apartment (top left) with Renaissance-style gouaches on the walls, gold-painted doors, and a black-and-white marble floor. The chandelier, a tasteful Italian-made design with a classic silhouette, is a restrained complement to so much richness. In Ned Marshall and Henry Norton's Long Island weekend home (bottom left), pale colors—including that of the painted floors—create an airy, beach-climate ambiance. In the dining area, an eighteenth-century Scandinavian chandelier pairs nicely with gilded Italian chairs and a modest, metal-based dining table. Opposite: Brazilian-born Sig Bergamin has spun a kaleidoscope of color and pattern in a fanciful dining room that mixes Anglo-Indian, Chinese lacquer, and Victorian bamboo furniture with shells, sea grass, baskets, and beads. All that's asked of the crystal chandelier is that it hang there and look pretty—which it does admirably.

In the library of his southern California home (left), architect Stephen Harby designed and built shelving perfectly proportioned for his books and collection of folk art. He finished it off with clever, do-it-yourself lighting elements— ordinary silver-topped incandescent bulbs in sockets recessed into wood panels between the uprights. These high-style, low-cost fixtures become part of the architecture. Opposite: Funky is as funky does in a 1960s-era northern California ranch house that sparkles with outdoorsy colors. Furnished in a combination of modern classics and secondhand treasures, it calls for lighting that's equally untraditional. In the dining room, a curved metal fixture serves as a wall-mounted sculpture as well as a spot of illumination.

In a California home furnished with midcentury modern furniture and the colors characteristic of the period, lighting fixtures from the same period were the natural choice: The interior boasts high ceilings, and the palette of brights and neutrals makes the most of the strong available natural light. Given the design parameters, it seemed only natural to focus on Isamu Noguchi designs; his sculptural lighting not only looks just right, but it also offers flattering illumination diffused through shades, and is relatively inexpensive. In the kitchen, left, a Noguchi globe hangs high, while plain pendant lights in inverted-tulip shapes spotlight the peninsula worktop. Lots of birch and polished wood floors are comfortable accompaniments to the classic Eames chairs at the dining table. The living room (opposite), is a comfortable Scandinavian-style arrangement of light woods and lively colors, accessorized with ceramics to suit. A tall Noguchi sculpture-cum-lamp and a funky orange lampshade complete the lively retro look.

DECK THE WALLS

Once simple mountings for torches or candles, sconces have long since been reborn as bulb-holding conveniences for built-in lighting, casting light in awkward spaces without taking up floor or table space. Today's versions are as varied as lamps, and just as decorative, offering the convenient options of uplight, downlight, or both. Moreover, they can be customized to disappear into the architecture—or the wallpaper.

Top left: In the hallway of fashion designer Geoffrey Beene's Hawaii house, only the open tops of a pair of custom built-in sconces reveal that they are anything other than architectural accents. Carrying out the designer's trademark black-and-white scheme, they supplement the recessed lighting overhead. Bottom left: William Diamond and Anthony Baratta built a framed niche in a red-and-white library and papered it with zingy plaid. They shaded the sconces to match; only the offset angle of the plaid and the soft light mark their presence. Opposite: Architect Stephen Harby mounted his own watercolor studies of classic and modern architecture on a corner wall, then lit them with a stylish but unobtrusive architectural sconce that emits light from the top, bottom, and center.

When a room calls for several kinds of lighting elements, should they match, contrast, or be altogether unrelated? The answer is, All of the above. Lighting decor should be chosen just like any other ornamental accessory.

Left: An extravagant two-story stair landing challenged designer Jeff Lincoln to glamorize a dark and difficult space. He met the problem head-on with an ingenious mixture of objects, art, and artful lighting. The glitter of a high and mighty eighteenth-century Venetian glass chandelier is reflected in a large mirror that also expands the space. On either side of the mirror, French wrought-iron sconces in the manner of Poillerat set off a symmetrical arrangement of tiny oil paintings. Beyond the Victorian-style circular settee stands a reproduction Giacometti brass floor lamp. Framing the setting, columns of iridescent sheer portieres are uplit with halogen bulbs for a radiant glow. Opposite: In the sumptuous foyer of a Palm Beach house whose owners rejected a pale, beachy look, designer Keith Irvine combined a nineteenth-century Italian painted tole chandelier with Louis XVI carved bronze doré sconces. On the console table is a pair of modern milk-glass hurricane candlesticks.

Light and space define the interiors of this elegantly understated home on an island off the coast of Florida, and lighting is one of the elements that makes it work. With its almost-all-white scheme perfectly suited to the oceanfront locale, the city-slick sophistication of the design is a pleasing change of pace for a neighborhood of conventionally conservative homes. Architects Peter Shelton and Lee Mindel created a beautifully balanced environment that is minimal but not stark, restful but not boring, bright but not glaring or uncomfortable. This last is a particularly noteworthy achievement in a climate with more than its fair share of tropical sun. Avoiding furniture that's simply for

clean living

A corner sectional sofa, upholstered in heavily textured off-white fabric, has the effect of a contrasting color accent against the pure white wall and floor. On the wall above it, an ingenious stretched-fabric light fixture stands in for artwork—which in this case it truly is. The low-standing halogen lamps are functional but unobtrusive, allowing the eye to focus on the wall piece.

show and surfaces that can't be touched, the livable interior scheme has a down-to-earth practicality that belies its sumptuous look.

Grand expanses of floor-to-ceiling glass take full advantage of the natural light; the overhang roof of the terrace provides a protective screen that allows daylight to flood the major rooms while shielding them from midday glare. The grandly proportioned public spaces suit the owners' fondness for large-scale entertaining, yet are equally comfortable for more intimate gatherings.

The furnishings are a contrast in tone and texture, from high-gloss white to smooth, matte surfaces to deep-textured beige and sandy tones. Occasional notes of color are more than sufficient to play off them. To

In the dining area (above left), light over the Frank Lloyd Wright table comes from a trio of classic Henningsen metal-shaded lamps. Above right: A collection of 1970s Italian glass vases on built-in display shelves provides discreet color accents in the white living room. Opposite: A pair of curvy Alvar Aalto chairs plays off Noguchi's tall pleated-paper Akari lamp. The floor-to-ceiling window looks onto the terrace and the palm trees beyond.

ensure that the interiors are just as inviting after dark, a combination of lighting elements is deployed throughout the rooms. These include modern classic fixtures by Henningsen, Noguchi, and Castiglioni, as well as conventional table lamps with modern lucite bases and standing lamps for reading. Additional lighting is built in—and altogether invisible. The understated glow these fixtures cast by evening is a pleasant change of pace from the brightness of the rooms by day.

The light-flooded living room (left) has 22-foot ceilings that enhance the grand proportions of its open, flowing space. The main seating arrangement, defined by a pale bordered rug on the white tile floor, combines white and sand-toned upholstery. Lighting fixtures are as light in design as they are effective in illumination: Glass jar lamps with light-spreading parchment shades anchor twin lacquered tables behind the sofas. Castiglioni's Arco floor lamp casts light from another plane. Above: Clustered in the entrance hall, four airy Noguchi Akari lamps cast diffused light while providing artistic accent.

directory of designers and architects

Audrey Alberts Design
Los Angeles, CA
(310) 477-8315

Barbara Barry
Los Angeles, CA
(310) 276-9977

Bruce Bernbaum
Bernbaum/Magadini
Architects
Dallas, TX
(214) 521-4531

R. Louis Bofferding Antiques
New York, NY
By appointment only
(212) 744-6725

Laura Bohn
LBDA, Inc.
New York, NY
(212) 645-3636

Nannette Brown, Ltd.
New York, NY
(212) 832-5400

Libby Cameron, LLC
Larchmont, NY
(914) 833-1414

Heather Cass, FAIA
Cass & Associates
Architects
Washington, DC
(202) 462-7663

Fu-Tung Cheng
Cheng Design &
Construction
Berkeley, CA
(510) 849-3272
www.chengdesign.com

John Chonka
TrueOrder Architects
Phoenix, AZ
(602) 256-2345

Pietro Cicognani, Ann Kalla
Cicognani Kalla
New York, NY
(212) 308-4811

Samantha Cole Interiors
Burlingame, CA
(650) 344-5400

Christopher Coleman Interior Design
Brooklyn, NY
(718) 222-8984

Monte Coleman
New York, NY
(212) 463-0085

Celeste Cooper/Repertoire
New York, NY
(212) 219-8159

Jack DeBartolo Jr., FAIA
DeBartolo Architects, Ltd.
Phoenix, AZ
(602) 264-6617

William Diamond, Anthony Baratta
Diamond Baratta Design
New York, NY
(212) 966-8892

Orlando Diaz-Azcuy Designs
San Francisco, CA
(415) 362-4500

T. Keller Donovan, Inc.
New York, NY
(212) 760-0537

Steven Ehrlich Architects
Culver City, CA
(310) 838-9700
www.s-ehrlich.com

Ken Foreman
Foreman Interior Designs
New York, NY
(212) 924-4503

Michael Formica Incorporated
New York, NY
(212) 620-0655
www.michaelformica.com

Albert Hadley Inc.
New York, NY
(212) 888-7979

Dorothy Haffner
New York, NY
(212) 337-3795

Mark Hampton, Inc.
New York, NY
(212) 753-4110

Amerlia T. Handegan, Inc.
Charleston, SC
(843) 722-9373

Stephen Harby
Santa Monica, CA
(310) 450-8239

Tiziana Hardy
New York, NY
(212) 777-5612

Kelly Harmon Interiors & Design
Santa Monica, CA
(310) 230-6717

Laura Hartman
Fernau & Hartman
Architects
Berkeley, CA
(510) 848-4480
www.fernauhartman.com

Jarrett Hedborg/Jeff Hiner Interior Design
Los Angeles, CA
(310) 271-1437

Ashley & Allegra Hicks
Allegra Hicks Design
London, England
011-44-20-7351-9696
www.allegrahicks.com

Keith Irvine
Irvine & Fleming, Inc.
New York, NY
(212) 888-6000

Hugh Newell Jacobsen, FAIA
Washington, D.C.
(202) 337-5200
www.hughjacobsen.com

Jed Johnson & Assoc., Inc.
New York, NY
(212) 489-7840

Kerry Joyce Assoc., Inc.
Los Angeles, CA
(323) 938-4442
www.kerryjoyce.com

Brian Killian & Co.
Birmingham, MI
(248) 645-9801

Todd Klein, Inc.
New York, NY
(212) 414-0001

Larry Laslo Designs
New York, NY
(212) 873-6797

**Christian Liaigre for
Holly Hunt**
Holly Hunt New York
New York, NY
(212) 755-6555
www.hollyhunt.com

Jeff Lincoln Interiors, Inc.
New York, NY
(212) 588-9500

**Paul Lubowicki,
Susan Lanier**
Lubowicki/Lanier Architects
El Segundo, CA
(310) 322-0211
www.lubowickilanier.com

**Mallory Marshall,
James Light**
Mallory James Interiors
Portland, ME
(207) 773-0180

Ned Marshall, Inc.
New York, NY
(212) 879-3672

Bobby McAlpine
McAlpine Tankersley
Architecture
Montgomery, AL
(334) 262-8315

Jack McCartney
McCartney Architects
Washington, DC
(202) 328-0200

**Antonio Morello,
Donato Savoie**
Studio Morsa
New York, NY
(212) 226-4324

Lynn Morgan Design
S. Norwalk, CT
(203) 854-5037

Brian Murphy, Inc.
New York, NY
(212) 545-0036
www.brianmurphyinc.com

Benjamin Noriega-Ortiz, LLC
New York, NY
(212) 343-9709
www.bnodesign.com

Henry Norton
Van Gregory and Norton
New York, NY
(212) 987-1170

Sandra Nunnerley, Inc.
New York, NY
(212) 826-0539

Thomas O'Brien
Aero Studios Ltd.
New York, NY
(212) 966-4700
www.aerostudios.com

Graham Phillips
Foster and Partners
London, England
011-44-20-7738-0455
www.fosterandpartners.com

**Rob Wellington Quigley,
FAIA**
San Diego, CA
(619) 232-0888

**Suzanne Rheinstein &
Associates**
W. Hollywood, CA
(310) 550-8900

John Saladino
Saladino Group, Inc.
New York, NY
(212) 752-2440

**DeBare Saunders,
Ronald Mayne**
Stingray Hornsby Interior
Design
Watertown, CT
(860) 274-2293

Stuart Schepps ASID
DSGN Interior Design Inc.
Cedar Grove, NJ
(973) 857-7722

**Peter Shelton,
Lee Mindel**
Shelton, Mindel & Assoc.
New York, NY
(212) 243-3939

Ken Shuttleworth
Foster and Partners
London, England
011-44-20-7738-0455
www.fosterandpartners.com

Alison Spear, AIA
New York, NY
(212) 439-8506
www.alisonspearaia.com

**Peter Stamberg,
Paul Aferiat**
Stamberg Aferiat
Architecture
New York, NY
(212) 255-4173
www.stambergaferiat.com

Emily Summers
Dallas, TX
(214) 871-9669

Alan Wanzenberg
Jed Johnson & Assoc., Inc.
New York, NY
(212) 489-7840

Paul Wiseman
The Wiseman Group
Interior Design, Inc.
San Francisco, CA
(415) 282-2880

Vicente Wolf Assoc., Inc.
New York, NY
(212) 465-0590

Buzz Yudell
Moore Ruble Yudell
Santa Monica, CA
(310) 450-1400

I	Robert Hiemstra
2	Scott Frances
5	Tim Street-Porter
6–7	Nigel Young
8	Paul Whicheloe
9	Fernando Bengoechea
10–11	Robert Lautman
12	Jeff McNamara
14	Christopher Irion
15	Tim Street-Porter
16	Langdon Clay
17	Victoria Pearson
18–21	Jeff McNamara
22–23	Elizabeth Zeschin
24	William Waldron
25	Michel Arnaud
26–29	William Waldron
30	Jeff McNamara
31	Thibault Jeanson
33	Minh & Wass (left)
	Paul Warchol (right)
34–35	Tim Street-Porter
36	Paul Whicheloe
37	Michel Arnaud
38	Jeff McNamara
39	William Waldron
40–43	Thibault Jeanson
44–47	Scott Frances
48–49	William Waldron
50–53	Scott Frances
54–57	Langdon Clay
58–59	Timothy Hursley
60–61	Tim Street-Porter
62	Robert Lautman
63	Gabi Zimmerman
64–65	Scott Frances
66	Tim Street-Porter
67	Laura Resen
68–73	Nigel Young
74	Peter Margonelli
76	Thibault Jeanson
77	Sam Gray
78	Scott Frances

79	Oberto Gili
80	Scott Frances
81	Scott Frances (left)
	Jonn Coolidge (right)
82–83	Peter Aaron/Esto
84–85	Robert Lautman
87	David Richmond
88–89	Peter Margonelli
90	Susie Cushner
91	Thibault Jeanson
92	Laura Resen
93	Jacques Dirand
94	Tim Street-Porter (top)
	Dominique Vorillon (bottom)
95	William Waldron
96–97	Jeff McNamara
98	Thibault Jeanson (top)
	Fernando Bengoechea (bottom)
99–100	Oberto Gili
101	Tim Street-Porter
102–03	William Waldron
104–05	Jeremy Samuelson
106	Scott Frances (top)
	Tim Street-Porter (bottom)
107	John Hall
108	Christopher Irion
109	Scott Frances
110	Peter Aaron/Esto
111	Scott Frances (top)
	Robert Hiemstra (bottom)
112	Balthazar Korab
113	Scott Frances
114	Laura Resen
115	Peter Margonelli (top)
	Tim Street-Porter (bottom)
116	Thibault Jeanson
118	Jonn Coolidge
119	Hichey Robertson
120	Richard Barnes
121	Jacques Dirand
122–25	Peter Aaron/Esto
126	Paul Warchol

128	Tom McWilliam
129	Vicente Wolf
130–31	Jacques Dirand
132	Scott Frances (top)
	Oberto Gili (bottom)
133	Scott Frances
134	Paul Whicheloe (left)
	Grey Crawford (right)
135	Barbara Stoeltie
136	Oberto Gili
137	Jacques Dirand
138–39	René Stoeltie
140–41	Scott Frances
142–43	Peter Margonelli
144	Mathew Millman
145	Santi Caleca
146–47	Oberto Gili
148	Thibault Jeanson
150	Paul Warchol
151	Dominique Vorillon
152	Robert Hiemstra
153	John Hall
154	Thibault Jeanson
155	Fernando Bengoechea
156	Fernando Bengoechea (top)
	Oberto Gili (bottom)
157	Scott Frances
158	Tim Street-Porter
159	Jeremy Samuelson
160–61	David Phelps
162	Scott Frances (top)
	Jonn Coolidge (bottom)
163	Tim Street-Porter
164	Pieter Estersohn
165	Thibault Jeanson
166–71	Jonn Coolidge
172	Laura Resen
175	Andrew Lautman
176	Oberto Gili

The room on page 1 was designed by Michael Formica;
page 2, Emily Summers and Bruce Bernbaum;
page 5, R. Louis Bofferding;
pages 6-7, Graham Phillips;
page 8, Tiziana Hardy;
pages 10-11, Hugh Newell Jacobsen;
page 172, Monte Coleman;
page 175, Heather Cass;
page 176, Michel Klein and Joel Fournier.